A Collection of 63 Anthems for the Church's Year

T0312625

The

New

Oxford

Easy

Anthem

Book

MUSIC DEPARTMENT

OXFORD
UNIVERSITY PRESS

OXFORD
UNIVERSITY PRESS

Great Clarendon Street, Oxford OX2 6DP, E
198 Madison Avenue, New York, NY10016

Oxford University Press is a department of the Unive
It furthers the University's aim of excellence in researc
and education by publishing worldwide i

Oxford New York
Auckland Cape Town Hong Kong Karachi
Kuala Lumpur Madrid Melbourne Mexico City Na
New Delhi Shanghai Taipei Toronto

With offices in

Argentina Austria Brazil Chile Czech Republic France (
Guatemala Hungary Italy Japan Poland Portugal Sing
South Korea Switzerland Thailand Turkey Ukraine Vie

Oxford is a registered trade mark of Oxford University Pr
in the UK and in certain other countries

ISBN 0-19-353318-9 978-0-19-353318-9 (pbk)
ISBN 0-19-335578-7 978-0-19-335578-1 (wiro)

Music and text origination by
Barnes Music Engraving Ltd., East Sussex
Printed in Great Britain on acid-free paper by
Halstan & Co. Ltd, Amersham, Bucks.

PREFACE

The *Oxford Easy Anthem Book* was published in 1957 as an accessible companion to the *Church Anthem Book* of 1933. Collecting together a number of pieces from the Oxford Easy Anthem series, it presented fifty easy pieces and a supplement of simple canticle and communion settings. Times and tastes change. While some pieces from the original selection rightly remain classics of the anthem repertoire, others no longer seem so relevant or have out-lived their musical appeal. The time seemed ripe for a brand new collection, reflecting the needs of church choirs today and introducing interesting and useful new repertoire.

The *New Oxford Easy Anthem Book* presents a broad range of easy and accessible anthems, mixing popular favourites from the Renaissance onwards with attractive new pieces, both with and without accompaniment. A significant proportion of the material is new. There are brand new anthems written specially for this collection, recently composed pieces establishing themselves in the repertoire, and newly commissioned arrangements of favourite pieces. Representing the very best contemporary church composers, such as John Rutter, Andrew Carter, Bob Chilcott, David Willcocks, Alan Bullard, Malcolm Archer, Simon Lole, and others, and adding favourite and little-known material from previous centuries, the book offers a great wealth of repertoire for church choirs everywhere.

When is an easy anthem easy? Views will differ about this and the pieces within this book, but various criteria have guided the selection. Vocally we have looked for lines which are uncomplicated and where ranges are comfortable. We have opted for SATB scoring, since not only does this allow for the inclusion of well-known established pieces, it also remains the scoring of aspiration, if not of fact, for the majority of church choirs. Wherever possible, however, divisi is kept to a minimum or is optional. There are also a few unison pieces and pieces that may be performed effectively with only two or three vocal parts. We have made the accompaniments as playable as possible, with a number simplified and most suitable for organ without pedals or for piano (pedal and manual indications are printed, but these may readily be adapted). The music is approachable and the language accessible. But although selected for technical ease, the pieces make no compromise of musical content, and reflect with integrity the richness of the musical response to Christian worship throughout the centuries.

English singing translations are provided for all the foreign-language pieces and full performance directions are given for the early repertoire. The pieces cover the whole of the Church's year with the exception of Christmas, for which many carol and other books exist. We have tried to invigorate most parts of the liturgical calendar with accessible recent material, either previously composed or brand new.

Grateful thanks are due to Helen Burrows in particular for her encouragement and many suggestions, and also to Peter Ward Jones, Peter Beaven, and Julian Elloway for repertoire ideas and comments.

INDEX OF TITLES AND FIRST LINES

Where first lines differ from titles, the former are shown in italics.

For anthems in Latin with English translations, both the Latin and English titles are shown in Roman.

THE CHURCH'S YEAR

* = also suitable for general use

for Derek Dorey and St Mildred's Addiscombe

1. Advent Message

Revelation 22: 20
and Isaiah 40: 3

Martin How
(b. 1931)

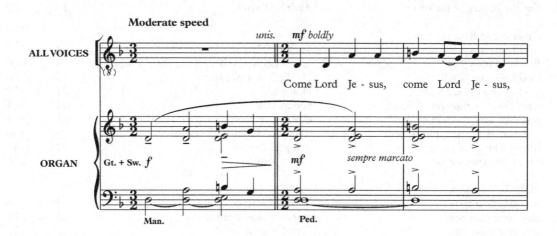

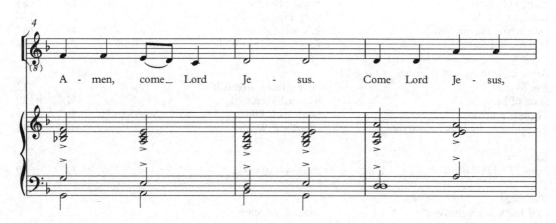

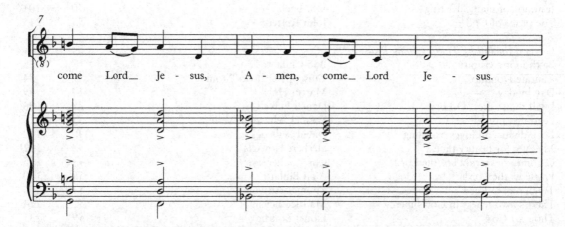

* This section should preferably be sung by a group. At the division, S./T. sing the higher notes, A./B. the lower. Alternatively, it may be sung by a soloist, in which case the top line only is sung.

* Sopranos and Tenors sing the higher notes.

*   Sopranos and Tenors divide as convenient.
** Top note Sopranos only.

for Rachel and Paul

2. And I saw a new heaven

Revelation 21: 1–2, 4

Malcolm Archer
(b. 1952)

This anthem was originally written in D major and may be transposed up to that key.

and there was no___ more sea,   and there was

no___ more sea,   for the first_ heaven and the first_ earth were passed___

___ a - way.___   And I saw___ a new

(organ double
voices ad lib.)

Man.

heaven_____ and a   new earth: for the   first_____ heaven_ and the

first_ earth   were   passed   a - way;_____   and there was

no___ more   sea,___ and there was   no___ more   sea,___ for the   first heaven and the

3. Ave Maria
(*Hail Virgin Mary*)

The Angelic Salutation

attrib. Jacob Arcadelt
(*c*.1500–68)
ed. Timothy Morris

All dynamics and tempo suggestions are editorial.

4. Ave verum corpus
(*Jesu, Lamb of God, Redeemer*)

Medieval sequence for Corpus Christi

Wolfgang Amadeus Mozart
(1756–91)

All dynamics are editorial.

5. Ave verum corpus
(*Blessed Word of God Incarnate*)

Medieval sequence for Corpus Christi

Robert Lucas Pearsall
(1795–1856)
ed. Richard Lyne

All dynamics and tempo suggestions are editorial, apart from the dynamics in bars 4 and 6, which are the composer's.

This edition is adapted from the one included in *Bread of Heaven*: Five Short Communion Anthems, Church Music Society Reprint No. 93.

6. Ave verum corpus
(*Jesu, Lamb of God, Redeemer*)

Medieval sequence for Corpus Christi

Camille Saint-Saëns
(1835–1921)

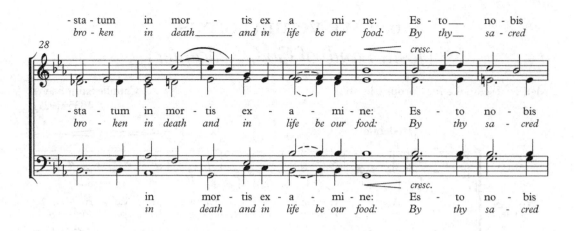

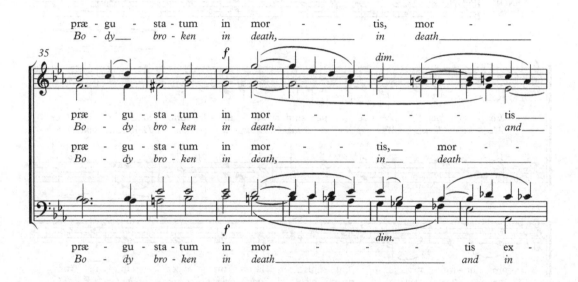

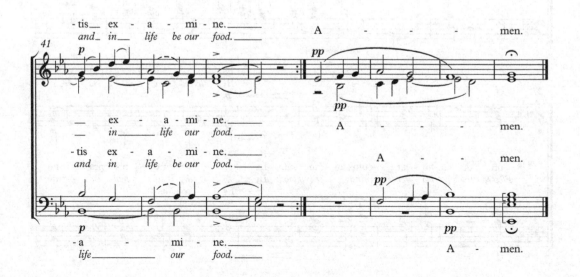

to the memory of William Chambers

7. Be thou my vision

Early Irish
tr. Mary Byrne (1880–1931)
versified Eleanor Hull (altered)
(1860–1935)

Bob Chilcott
(b. 1955)

A version of this piece (BC43) with piano accompaniment is available separately (ISBN 978–0–19–343292–5).

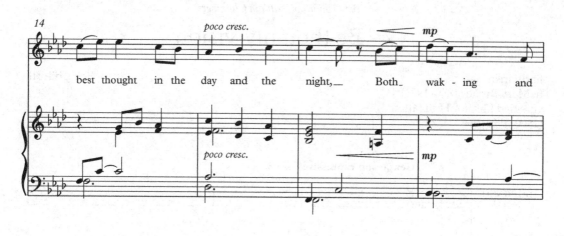

best thought in the day and the night,___ Both___ wak - ing and

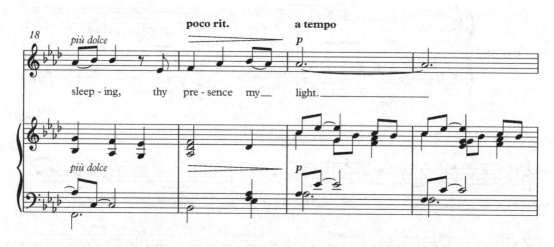

sleep - ing, thy pre - sence my___ light._____

Be___ thou my___

Be___ thou my vi - sion, O___ Lord of my

Be___ thou my

Be___ thou my

8. Brother James' Air
(*The Lord's my Shepherd*)

The Scottish Psalter, 1650 (*v.*5 altered)
based on Psalm 23

James Leith MacBeth Bain
(1860–1925)
arr. Alan Bullard
(b. 1947)

* From here until the end:
  1. Organ manuals only — play as written.
  2. Piano — add L.H. lower octave.
  3. Organ with pedals — use pedals (with 16') for bottom line; in upper stave play downstemmed notes an octave lower with left hand.

9. Cantate Domino
(*Come ye with joyfulness*)

Psalm 149: 1–2
tr. Francis Jackson
(b. 1917)

Giuseppe Ottavio Pitoni
(1657–1743)

All dynamics and tempo suggestions are editorial. To lengthen this anthem, bars 1–18 and 19–40 may each be repeated.

10. Christ is our Cornerstone

7th- or 8th-cent. Latin
tr. John Chandler (1806–76)
and Psalm 118: 22

David Thorne
(b. 1950)

for Alan Thurlow and the Choir of Chichester Cathedral

11. Christ the Lord is risen again!

Michael Weisse
(*c.*1480–*c.*1530)
tr. Catherine Winkworth
(1827–78)

Anthony Foster
(b. 1926)

This piece (X280) is also available separately (ISBN 978–0–19–343081–5).

12. Come, Holy Ghost

John Cosin
(1594–1672)
based on Veni, Creator Spiritus

Thomas Attwood
(1765–1838)

Larghetto

SOPRANO: Come, Ho - ly_ Ghost, our souls in - spire, And light - en with ce - les - tial_ fire; Thou the a - noint - ing Spi - rit art, Who dost thy sev - en - fold gifts im - part:_ Thy bless - ed unc - tion from_ a - bove_ Is

13. Come, ye faithful

John of Damascus
(*c.*675–*c.*750)
tr. J. M. Neale
(1818–66)

R. S. Thatcher
(1888–1957)

With movement

ALL VOICES — *unis.* *f*
Come, ye faith - ful,

ORGAN — *f*

Ped.

raise_ the strain   Of   tri - um - phant glad - ness;   God hath

brought his Is - ra - el   In - to joy from sad - ness;   'Tis_ the

mf

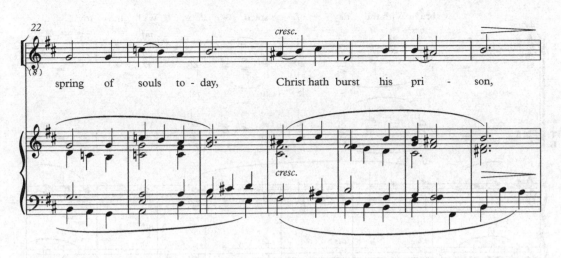

spring of souls to-day, Christ hath burst his pri - son,

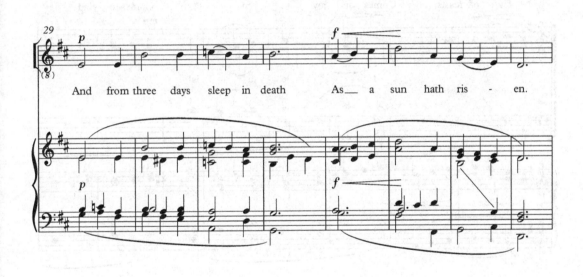

And from three days sleep in death As_ a sun hath ris - en.

SOPRANOS *p*

Now the queen of sea -

14. Day by day

Richard of Chichester
(1197–1253)

Martin How
(b. 1931)

15. Drop, drop, slow tears

Phineas Fletcher
(1582–1650)

Orlando Gibbons
(1583–1625)
arr. David Blackwell
(b. 1961)

16. Far away, what splendour comes this way?

Mary Barham Johnson
(1895–1996)

attrib. Jean-Baptiste Lully (1632–87)
arr. Georges Bizet (1838–75)
adapted Hugh Keyte & Andrew Parrott

All dynamics and tempo suggestions are editorial. Verse 1 may be sung in unison.

har - ness of the ca - mels; O rich and fair Are the
ba - by in a man - ger? O tell me why, In a

robes they wear, And on their tur-bans glit - ter jew - els rare.
sta - ble nigh, They wor - ship him who on a cross will die?

2. Kings, all three, such splen - did men must be, For

2. Kings, all three, such splen - did men must

each is bril-liant as a gold - en sun - rise;_ Kings, all three, such

be, For each is bril-liant as a gold - en sun - rise; Kings, all

splen - did men   must be,   Who   on   white   stal - lions ride a

three,   such splen - did men   must be,   Who   on   white

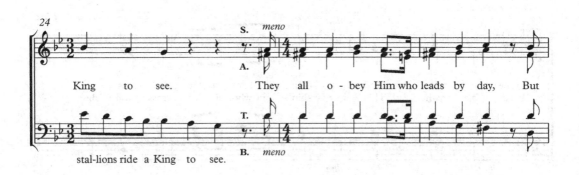

King   to   see.   They   all   o - bey Him who leads by day,   But

stal-lions ride a King   to   see.

ev - ery night   by a   star they have been guid - ed,   They   all   o - bey Him who

leads   by   day;   His   long   white   beard is seen from   far   a - way.

17. Fear not, O land

Joel 2: 21–6

William H. Harris
(1883–1973)

fruit, the fig tree and the vine do yield their___ strength.

SOPRANOS *f*

Man.

Gt.

Ped.

Be glad_____ then, ye chil-dren of Zi- on, and re - joice in the

f

S.

A. *f*

f

rit.   **SOPRANOS**
p

Lord your God._____

The

rit.

f

dim.

18. For all thy saints

Richard Mant
(1776–1848)

Alan Bullard
(b. 1947)

With stately ceremony ($\downarrow$ = *c*.60)

ALL VOICES

For all thy saints, O Lord,— Who strove in

ORGAN
(or piano)

Man.

thee to live, Who fol-lowed thee, o-beyed, a-dored, Our grate-ful hymn re-

S.
A.

- ceive.

For all thy

T.
B.

f grandly

f grandly

f grandly

Ped.

for the dedication of Northridge United Methodist Church, California, December 1991
Commissioned by Malcolm and Margaret Sears to celebrate their Fiftieth Wedding Anniversary

19. For the beauty of the earth

Folliott Sandford Pierpoint (altered)
(1837–1917)

Andrew Carter
(b. 1939)

For the beauty of the earth is one movement from the longer work *Great is the Lord* published by Morning Star Music Publishers of St Louis.

A version of this piece (U173) for unison upper voices, piano, and flute is also available separately (ISBN 978-0-19-342072-4).

Fa-ther, un-to thee_ we raise_____ This our joy-ful hymn of praise.

Solo Flutes

Solo off

(organ double
voices ad lib.)

2. For the

beau - ty of each hour   Of the   day   and of the night,   Hill and   vale,   and tree and

heart   and brain's de - light,   For the   mys - tic   har - mo - ny   Link-ing

sense   to sound and   sight:

4. For the   joy   of hu-man   love,_____

Solo Flutes

cresc.

poco *f*

poco *f*

Solo off

(organ double voices ad lib.)

Bro-ther, sis - ter, par-ent, child, Friends on earth and friends a - bove, For all

gen-tle thoughts and_ mild:_ Fa - ther un-to thee_ we raise_____

This our joy-ful hymn of praise.

5. For each per - fect gift of thine   To our race   so free-ly

giv'n,   Gra-ces hu - man and di-vine,   Flow'rs of earth and buds of heav'n:

Fa-ther un-to thee we raise_____   This our joy-ful hymn_   of praise!

20. God be in my head

From a Book of Hours
(Sarum, 1514)

H. Walford Davies
(1869–1941)

All dynamics and tempo suggestions are editorial.

for the choir of St Peter's, Thorner

21. God be in my head

From a Book of Hours
(Sarum, 1514)

Philip Wilby
(b. 1949)

* Breathe when necessary.

in__ my look-ing; God be in my mouth, and
God__ be in my mouth,__
God be in my mouth, and
God__ be in my mouth, and

Ped.

in__ my speak-ing; God be in my heart, and
__ and in my speak-ing;__ God__ be in my heart,
in__ my speak-ing; God be in my heart, and
in my speak-ing;__ God__ be in my heart,__

22. God so loved the world

John 3: 16

John Stainer
(1840–1901)
from *The Crucifixion*, 1887

23. Holy, holy, holy

Franz Schubert
(1797–1828)
adapted from the *Deutsche Messe*, 1826

for Berkley

24. Holy Spirit, truth divine

Samuel Longfellow (altered)
(1819–92)

Andrew Carter
(b. 1939)

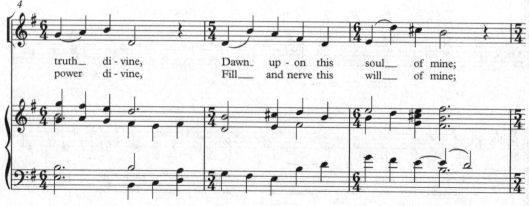

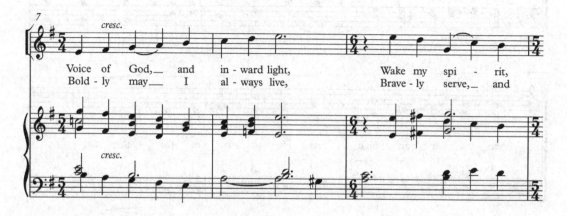

This piece (A446) is available separately (ISBN 978–0–19–350500–1).

clear my sight,   wake my spi - rit,   clear my sight.
glad - ly live,   brave - ly serve, and   glad - ly live.

Ped.

S.
A.

2. Ho   ly   Spi - rit,
4. Ho   ly   Spi - rit,

T.
B.

mp

mf

(organ double
voices ad lib.)

love___ di - vine,___   Glow___ with - in   this   heart___ of mine;___
peace_ di - vine,___   Still___ this rest - less heart___ of mine;___

cresc.

Kin -
Speak_

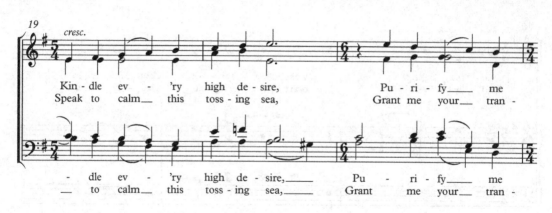

Kin - dle ev - 'ry high de - sire, Pu - ri - fy___ me
Speak to calm___ this toss - ing sea, Grant me your___ tran -

- dle ev - 'ry high de - sire,___ Pu - ri - fy___ me
- to calm___ this toss - ing sea,___ Grant me your___ tran -

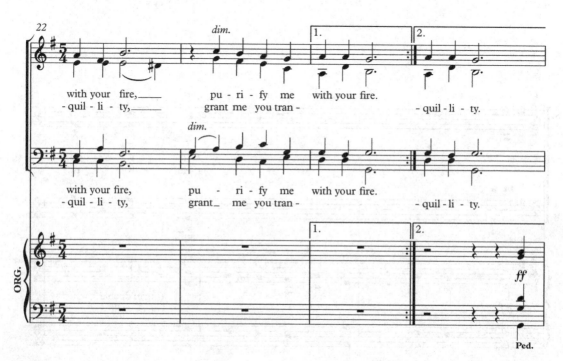

with your fire,___ pu - ri - fy me with your fire.
- quil - li - ty,___ grant me you tran - - quil - li - ty.

with your fire, pu - ri - fy me with your fire.
- quil - li - ty, grant___ me you tran - - quil - li - ty.

SOPRANO DESCANT *f*

5. Ho - ly Spi - rit,

ALL OTHER VOICES *f*

5. Ho - ly Spi - rit,

25. Hosanna to the Son of David

Matthew 21: 9

David Halls
(b. 1963)

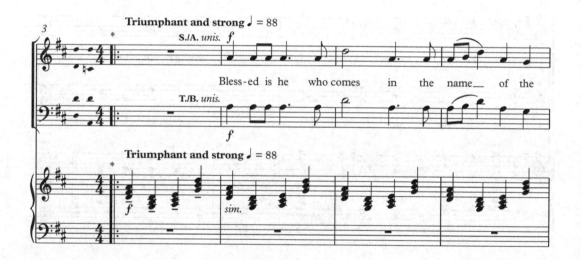

* optional repeat.

* optional repeat.

26. How brightly beams the morning star!

Philipp Nicolai (1556–1608)
and Johann Schlegel (1721–93)
tr. Catherine Winkworth (1827–78)

Dirck Janszoon Sweelinck
(1591–1652)

All dynamics and tempo suggestions are editorial.

27. I give you a new commandment

John 13: 34–5

Peter Aston
(b. 1938)

* This anthem may effectively be sung by any combination of voices, dividing as appropriate.

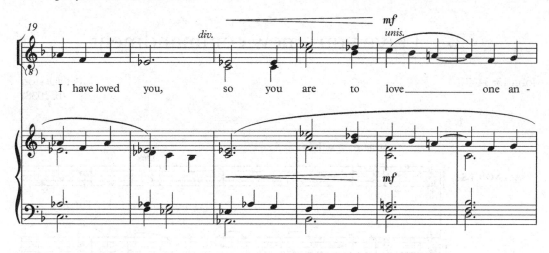

I have loved you, so you are to love_____ one an -

- o - ther._____   I give you a

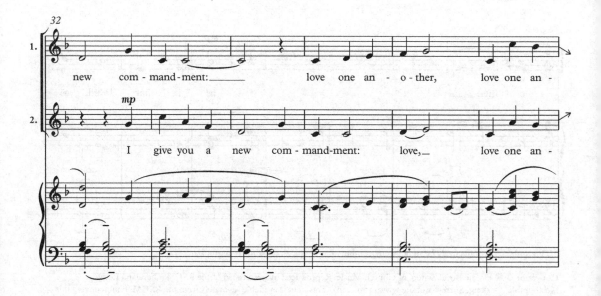

1. new com - mand - ment:_____ love one an - o - ther, love one an -

2. I give you a new com - mand - ment: love,__ love one an -

28. I will thank thee, O Lord

Psalm 86: 12–13

Daniel Purcell
(*c.*1660–1717)
ed. Christopher Dearnley
(1930–2000)

All dynamics and tempo suggestions are editorial.

ev - er - more: For   great   is   thy
              For   great   is   thy   mer   -   cy   to'ards me,

For   great   is   thy   mer   -   cy
(bass)

For   great   is   thy   mer   -   cy   to'ards me,

mer   -   cy   to'ards   me,   great   is   thy   mer - cy,
great   is   thy   mer   -   cy,   great   is   thy   mer - cy,

to'ards   me,   great   is   thy   mer   -   cy   to'ards   me,

cresc.

great,   great,_   great   is   thy   mer   -   cy___   to'ards   me,

cresc.

f   **rall.**

great,   great   is   thy   mer   -   cy___   to'ards   me.

f

29. If ye love me

John 14: 15–17

Thomas Tallis
(*c*.1505–85)

All dynamics and tempo suggestions are editorial.

30. Jesu, joy of man's desiring

Martin Jahn
(*c*.1620–*c*.1682)
tr. Robert Bridges
(1844–1930)

J. S. Bach
(1685–1750)

1. Je - su, joy___ of man's___ de -
2. Through the way___ where Hope___ is

All dynamics and tempo suggestions are editorial.

* The original notation of has been simplified throughout to reflect the correct realisation of Baroque performance practice.

round____ thy____ throne.
joys____ un - known.

31. Jesu, the very thought of thee

12th-cent. Latin
tr. Edward Caswall (altered)
(1814–78)

Simon Lole
(b. 1957)

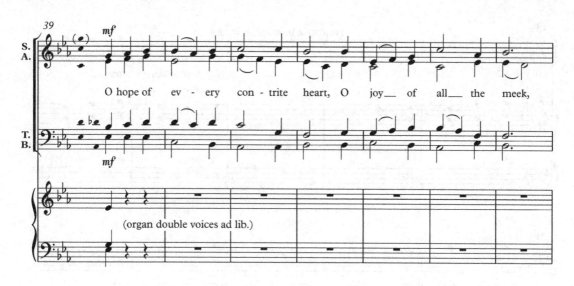

O hope of ev - ery con - trite heart, O joy__ of all__ the meek,

(organ double voices ad lib.)

To those who fall,__ how kind__ thou art,__ How good to those who seek!

TENORS & BASSES *unis.* *mf*

But what to those__ who

find? Ah, this Nor tongue nor pen can show;_____

The love___ of Je - sus, what___ it is None

but___ his loved_ ones know.

for Kirk in the Hills Presbyterian Church, Bloomfield Hills, Michigan

32. Jesu, the very thought of thee

12th-cent. Latin
tr. Edward Caswall (altered)
(1814–78)

Glenn L. Rudolph
(b. 1951)

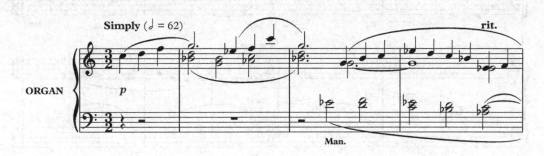

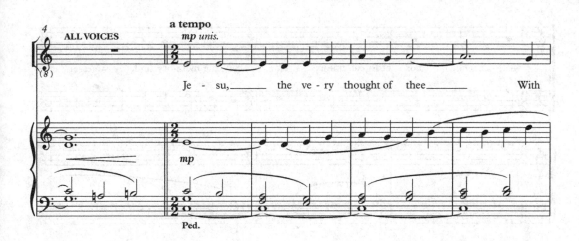

see, And in thy pre - sence rest._____   Nor

voice can sing,   nor   heart can frame,   Nor   can the mem-ory find, A sweet-er

sound   than thy blest   name,   O   Sa - viour of___ man -

33. Joy is come!

Andrew Carter

14th-cent. German melody
arr. Andrew Carter
(b. 1939)

1. Joy is come! Eas-ter-tide! Sing we all far and wide, See the stone rolled a-side, Christ our Lord is ris - en, Burst-ing from his pri - son. Let the sound, sound, sound, Ring a-round,

An unaccompanied version of this piece (A451) is available separately (ISBN 978–0–19–350506–3).

round, round,   And the song   now re-bound: Christ the Lord is   ris - en!

2. Joy is   come!

Eas - ter   Day!__   Join   the   dance,__   ho - mage pay,   Christ the   Lord__

lights our way,   From the tomb now   break - ing,__ Sa - tan's pow - er

shak - ing.   Let the song,   song, song,   E - cho long,   long,   long,

Shout it loud,__ sing it strong: Christ the Lord is   ris - en!

3. Joy is come! Eas - ter morn! With your Lord

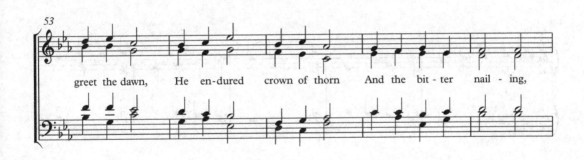

greet the dawn,   He en-dured   crown of thorn   And the bit - ter   nail - ing,

Faith-ful and un - fail - ing.   Ti-dings tell,   tell,   tell,   Chant it well,

well,   well,   Ris - en   Christ   in   us dwell,   O'er the cross pre - vail - ing.

Man.

Ped.

4. Eas - ter   joy   may   we bring,

Wel-come, Lord, hea-ven's King, Win-ter turns in-to spring,

Dark-ness o-ver-tak - ing, And our spi-rits wak - ing.

S. Prais - es flow,___ flow,___ flow, Voi - ces grow,___

A. Prais - es flow, flow, flow, Voi - ces grow,

T. Prais - es flow,___ flow,___ flow, Voi - ces grow,___

B. Prais - es flow, flow, flow, Voi - ces grow,

34. King of all ages, throned on high

10th-cent. Latin
tr. Mount Saint Bernard Abbey

Paul Isom
(b. 1959)

This piece (E175) is available separately (ISBN 978–0–19–335623–8)

SOPRANOS & ALTOS *unis.*

mp

Then at your com - ing on___ the clouds With shin - ing

Man.

strength to be___ our judge,   *mf*   Can - cel the debt we

Ped.

owe___ you still, Give back___ the glo - ry we___ have

lost.

35. Lead me, Lord

Psalms 5: 8, 4: 9

Samuel Sebastian Wesley
(1810–76)

ORGAN

SOPRANO or ALTO (SOLO or TUTTI)

Lead me, Lord, lead me in thy right - eous-ness,

make thy way plain be - fore my face.

36. Let us now praise famous men

Ecclesiasticus 44

Ralph Vaughan Williams
(1872–1958)
ed. Lionel Dakers

And some there be, which have no me-mo-ri-al; who are
pe-rished, as though they had ne-ver been. Their bo-dies are
bu-ried in peace; but their name liv-eth for ev-er-
- more.

for Richard Lloyd

37. Litany to the Holy Spirit

Robert Herrick
(1591–1674)

Peter Hurford
(b. 1930)

This piece (E164) is available separately (ISBN 978–0–19–351150–7). The original version (U37) for solo soprano and piano or organ is also available separately (ISBN 978–0–19–341937–7).

3. When___ the house doth sigh and weep,

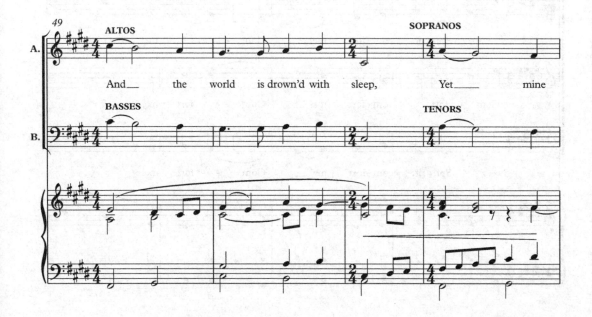

And___ the world is drown'd with sleep, Yet___ mine

* A few tenors (or basses).

38. Lord, for thy tender mercy's sake

from J. Bull
Christian Prayers and Holy Meditations (1568)

attrib. Richard Farrant
(*c.*1530–80)
or John Hilton
(*c.*1560–1608)

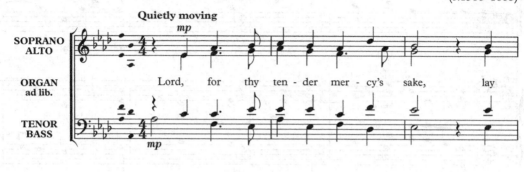

Lord, for thy ten-der mer-cy's sake, lay

not our sins to our charge, but for-give that is

past, and give us grace to a-mend our sin-ful___ lives:

to de-cline from sin and in-cline to vir-tue,

that we may

* All dynamics and tempo suggestions are editorial.

This piece (OCCO31) is available separately (ISBN 978–0–19–341805–9).

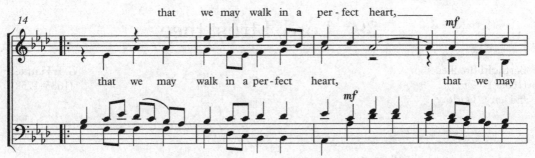

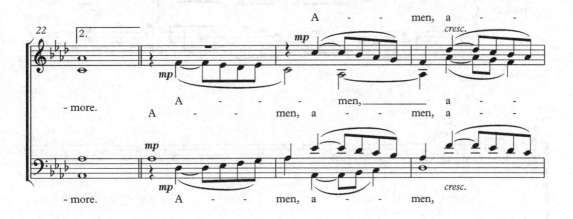

39. Lord, I trust thee

Barthold Brockes
(1680–1747)
tr. Denys Darlow

G. F. Handel
(1685–1759)

This piece (E110) is available separately (ISBN 978–0–19–351095–1).

joy— and end - less peace. When the breath of   life   has   left—

me,   May my   soul be   blend-ed   with___ thee.

for the 50th anniversary of the Sewanee Church Music Conference, USA

40. Love divine, all loves excelling

Charles Wesley
(1707–88)

David Willcocks
(b. 1919)

* 'Jesu' in Wesley's original.

This piece (E176) is available separately (ISBN 978–0–19–335633–7)

ne - ver, Ne-ver more thy tem-ples leave. Thee we would be al-ways

Thee we would be al-ways

bless - ing,   Serve thee as thy hosts a - bove;

bless - ing, Serve thee as   thy hosts a - bove;   Pray, and praise thee, with-out

bless - ing,   Serve thee as thy hosts a - bove;

ceas - ing,   Glo - ry in thy per-fect   love.

ORG.

Ped.

41. Loving Shepherd of thy sheep

Jane E. Leeson
(1807–82)

Philip Ledger
(b. 1937)

42. My eyes for beauty pine

Robert Bridges
(1844–1930)

Herbert Howells
(1892–1983)

This piece (A14) is available separately (ISBN 978–0–19–350112–6).

One splen - - dour thence is shed from all the stars a-bove: 'Tis nam - ed when God's name is said, 'Tis Love, 'tis heaven - ly Love.

43. O come, ye servants of the Lord

Verses from Psalm 113

Christopher Tye
(*c*.1505–73)

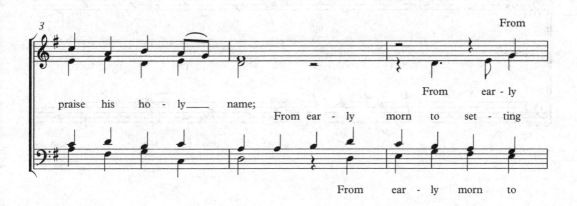

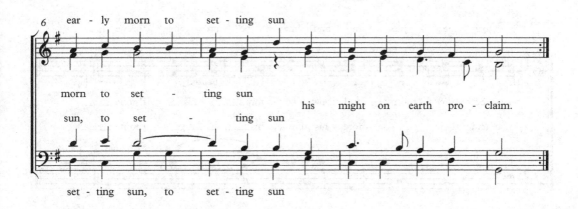

His laws are just, and glad the heart; He makes his mer - cies

Ye prin - ces come,____

Ye prin - ces come, ye peo - ple too, and

known: Ye prin - ces come, ye peo - ple, peo - ple too,

Ye prin - ces come, ye peo - ple too,   and

— ye peo - ple too, and bow be - fore his throne.____

bow be - fore his throne, and bow be - fore____ his__ throne.____

and bow be - fore his throne, his____ throne.____

bow be - fore his throne, and bow be - fore his throne.____

44. O salutaris Hostia No. 3
(*O saving Victim*)

Thomas Aquinas (1227–74)
tr. Edward Caswall (1814–78)

Edward Elgar
(1857–1934)
ed. J. H. T. Hooke

45. O Saviour of the world

Antiphon of the Holy Cross

John Goss
(1800–80)

* All small notes are for the optional organ accompaniment.

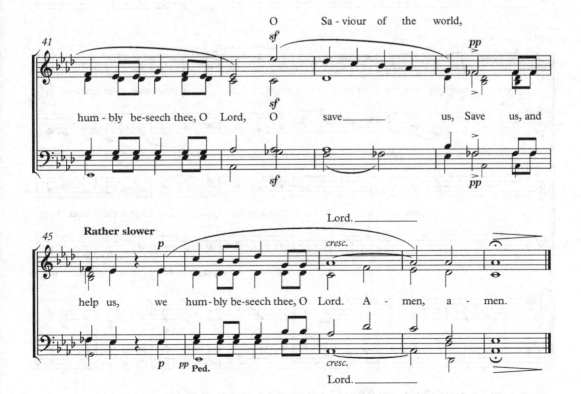

46.   O taste and see

Psalm 34: 8

Ralph Vaughan Williams
(1872–1958)

This piece may be sung in the key of G flat. It is available separately (ISBN 978–0–19–353511–4).

47. O Thou, whose all-redeeming might

8th-cent. hymn
tr. R M Benson SSJE (altered)
(1824–1915)

Plainsong melody, mode viii
arr. David Blackwell
(b. 1961)

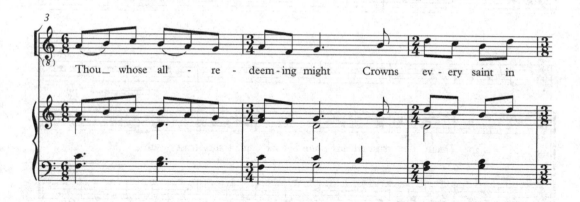

day Hear us,— good Je - su, while we pray.

TENORS
& BASSES *unis.*   *mp*   *div.*

2. Con - tend - ing for— thy ho - ly name Thy ser - vants earned their

saint - ly fame, Which pi - ous hearts with praise re - vere In

con - stant mem - ory year by year.

p   *legato*

(Man.)

3. Earth's fleet - ing joys___ they count-ed naught,   For

high - er, tru - er   joys___ they   sought,   And   now, with An - gels

round thy   throne,   Un - fad - ing trea - sures   are their own.   4. O

(organ ad lib.)

grant__ that we,__ most gra - cious God, May fol - low in the

steps____ they trod; And, freed from ev - ery

stain__ of sin, As they__ have won__ may al - so win.

thee,   O   Christ,   our   lov - ing   King,   All   glo - ry, praise, and

thanks_   we   bring;   Whom   with   the   Fa - ther   we   a -

-dore,   And   Ho - ly   Ghost_   for   ev - er - more.

A   -   men,_____   a   -   men,_____

_   a _   men._____

48. O vos omnes
(Is it nothing to you)

Lamentations 1: 12

Henrique Carlos Corrêa
(1680–?1752)

All dynamics and tempo suggestions are editorial.

49. People, look East

Eleanor Farjeon
(1881–1965)

Besançon carol melody
arr. Malcolm Archer
(b. 1952)

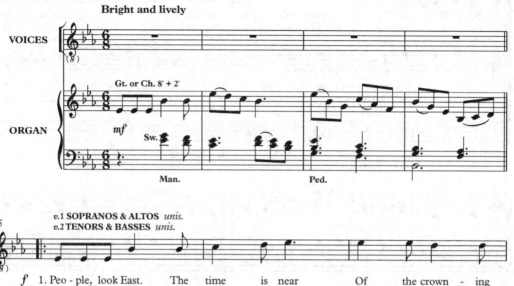

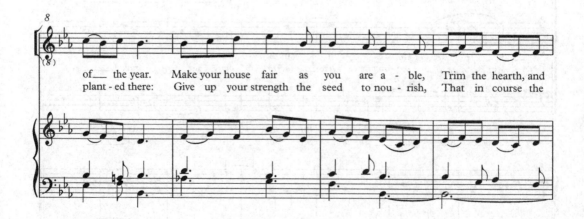

This piece (E174) is available separately (ISBN 978–0–19–335624–5).

set__ the ta - ble. Peo-ple, look East, and sing to-day: Love the Guest is
flower may flou - rish. Peo-ple, look East, and sing to-day: Love the Rose is

Sw.

Man.

on__ the way.
on__ the way.

Gt. or Ch. 8' + 2'

1. *mf*
2. *mp*

Man.

Ped.

mp

3. Stars, keep the   watch.__ When   night__ is dim_____   One more light   the

mp

(organ double voices ad lib.)

bowl___ shall brim,   Shin - ing be - yond   the   frost - y wea - ther,

Bright   as sun___ and   moon___ to - ge - ther.   Peo - ple, look East,___ and

sing___ to - day: Love   the Star   is   on___ the way.

(organ double voices ad lib.)

Gt. and Sw. (Sw. reeds)   *mf*

Man.

4. An-gels, an-nounce to man and beast Him who com - eth from_ the East.

Set ev - ery peak and val - ley hum-ming With the word, the Lord is com - ing.

Peo-ple, look East, and sing_ to-day: Love the Lord is on_ the way.

50.   Praise ye the Lord

Psalm 148: 1–3

Alan Bullard
(b. 1947)

heights.

Praise   ye   the   Lord!

allargando

Piano 8va bassa

51. Song of Mary
(*My Lord and Saviour is my song*)

Mary Holtby
after Luke 1: 46–55

Richard Shephard
(b. 1949)

The original, fuller version of the organ part is published, with the choir parts, as a separate leaflet, A442,
(ISBN 978–0–19–343248–2).

a - ni-ma me - a   Do - mi - num.

(Man.)

SOPRANOS & ALTOS *unis.*

My name shall live from age to age,   And   ev - 'ry tongue his

ser - vant bless,_____   For   mer - cy is their   he - ri - tage_____

_____ Whose hearts_____ the Ho - ly   One   con - fess.

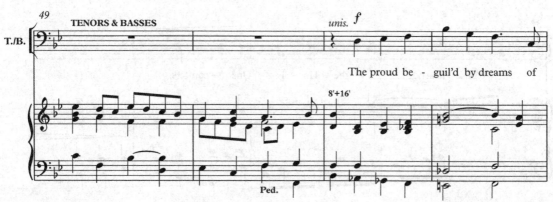

pow'r Di - vi - ded and de - gra - ded lie:_____ He casts them down from

throne and tow'r_____ And stoops_____ to lift the hum - ble high.

Mag - ni - fi-cat,   Mag - ni - fi-cat,   Mag -

Mag - ni - fi-cat,   Mag - ni - fi-cat, Mag -

With all the el-ders of our race, And those un-born who seek this birth,_____ I sing the glo-ry of his grace_____ Who brings_____ e-ter-ni-ty to earth.

52. Star of the East
(*Brightest and best*)

Reginald Heber
(1783–1826)

Alan Bullard
(b. 1947)

Bright - est and best of the sons of the morn - ing,

Dawn on our dark - ness and lend us thine aid;

* Omit lower part, if solo.

Star of the East, the ho - ri - zon a - dorn - ing,

Guide where our in - fant Re - deem - er is laid.

Cold on his cra - dle the
Cold_____ the

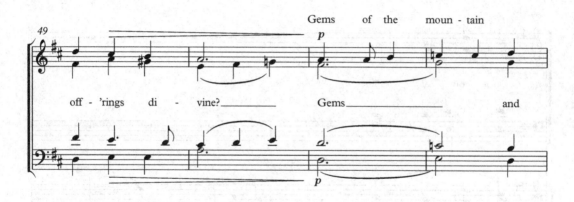

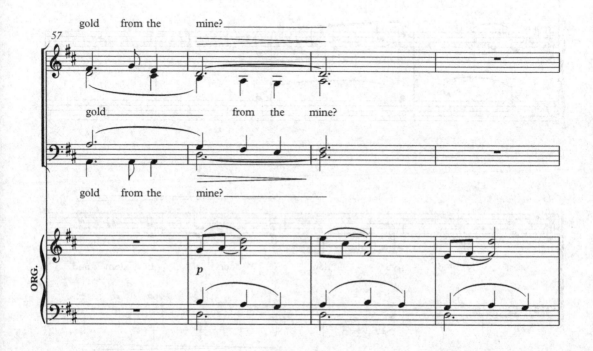

Vain - ly we of - fer each am - ple ob -

- la - tion, Vain - ly with gifts would his fa - vour se - cure;

Rich - er by far is the heart's a - do - ra - tion,

Dear-er___ to God are the prayers of the poor.

Bright - est and best of the sons of the morn - ing,

Dawn on our dark - ness and lend us thine aid;

53. Teach me, O Lord

Psalm 119: 33

Thomas Attwood
(1765–1838)

22

end, and I____ shall keep it un-to____ the____ end.

p

p

p

Man.

27

Teach me, O Lord, teach me, O Lord,

mf

mf

Teach me, O Lord, O Lord, the

mf

mf

Ped.

31

way of thy sta-tutes, and I shall keep it, and

Man.   Ped.   Man.

54. The Lord goes up

From Stanbrook Abbey Hymnal

Malcolm Archer
(b. 1952)
based on a French church melody

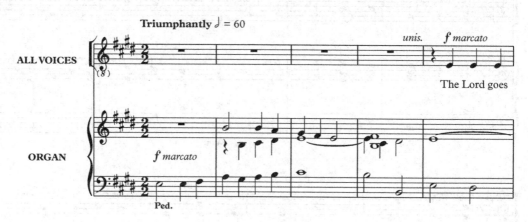

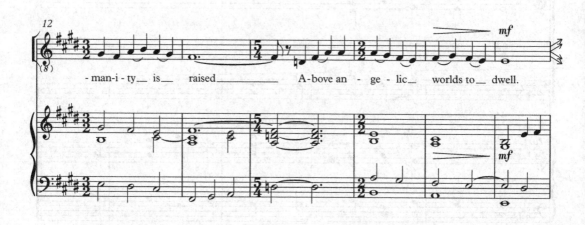

him,   And ev - ery   tear___ be___ wiped a - way.

O God, our   Fa-ther, hear our

prayer: With Christ, our___ Lord, your on - ly   Son,   Send forth the

for Bishop Thomas McMahon and the people of the Diocese of Brentwood

55. The peace of God

Book of Common Prayer (1662)

John Rutter
(b. 1945)

This piece (E157) is also available separately (ISBN 978–0–19–351143–9). A version for upper voices (W110) is also available separately (ISBN 978–0–19–342609–2).

for the Chapel Choir of Birkenhead School

56. There is no rose

Graham J. Ellis
(b. 1952)

15th-cent. carol

The original full version of this anthem is available from the Church Music Society (Publication 028).

Heav'n and earth in lit - tle space: *Res_ mi - ran - da.

3. By that_ rose we may well see There be one God in per - sons three:_

(organ double voices ad lib.)

**Pa - res_ for - ma, pa - res_ for - ma, pa - res for - ma.

Pa - res_ for - ma, pa - res, pa - res for - ma.

Pa - res_ for - ma, pa - res for - ma,_ pa - res for - ma.

*   'A wonderful thing'
** 'Of the same form'

4. Then leave we all this world-ly mirth, And fol-low we this joy-ous birth; *Trans-*

(Hum)

Man.   Ped.

- e - a - mus, trans - e - a - mus, trans - e - a - mus.
Trans - e - a - mus,

Trans - e - a - mus,

Trans - e - a - mus, trans - e - a - mus, trans - e - a - mus.

* 'Let us go'

57. There's a wideness in God's mercy

Frederick William Faber (*v.7 altered*)
(1814–63)

Maurice Bevan
(b. 1921)

The original hymn-tune is available from Cathedral Music (King Charles Cottage, Racton, Chichester, West Sussex PO18 9DT).

sor - rows Are more felt   than up in heaven;   There is   no   place where earth's

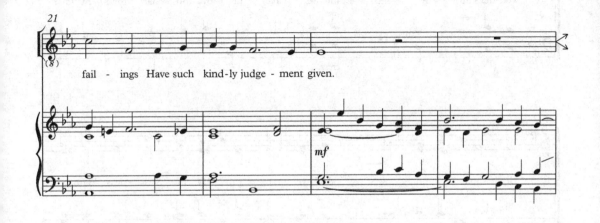

fail - ings Have such kind-ly judge - ment given.

3. For the   love   of God is broad - er Than the

(organ double voices ad lib.)

58. This joyful Eastertide

G. R. Woodward
(1848–1934)

Dutch carol
arr. Charles Wood
(1866–1926)

in memory of Jean

59. Thou art God

David Adam
(b. 1936)

Lionel Bourne
(b. 1960)

Thou art the peace of all things calm, Thou art the place to hide from

harm, Thou art the light that shines in＿ dark, Thou art the heart's e - ter - nal

A version of this piece (E171) with optional parts for flute and oboe is available separately (ISBN 978–0–19–351158–3).
A version for upper voices (E170) is also available separately (ISBN 978–0–19–351157–6).

spark,   Thou art the   door that's o - pen   wide,   Thou art the   guest   who waits in -

-side,   Thou art the stran-ger   at the door,   Thou art the   call - ing of the   poor.

Thou art the peace   of all things

S.
A.

Ah

60. Thou knowest, Lord

From the Burial Service,
Book of Common Prayer

Henry Purcell
(1659–95)

All dynamics, tempo, and articulation marks are editorial.

mer - ci - ful___ Sa - viour,   Thou most wor - thy   Judge e - ter - nal,

suf - fer us   not,   suf - fer us not,   at our

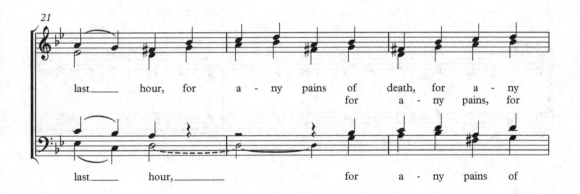

last___ hour,   for   a - ny   pains   of   death,   for   a - ny
             for   a - ny   pains,   for

last___ hour,_____   for   a - ny   pains   of

pains   of   death, to   fall,   to   fall from   thee.   A - men.
a - ny   pains of   death,

death,_____ to   fall,

for John Preston Bell and the choir of Meopham Parish Church

61. Thy perfect love

15th cent.

John Rutter
(b. 1945)

This anthem may be performed in a shortened form, beginning at bar 37.
This piece (E137) is available separately (ISBN 978–0–19–351122–4). There is also an accompaniment scored for strings.
Score and parts are on hire.

62. Virgin-born, we bow before thee

Reginald Heber
(1783–1826)

Charles F. Waters
(1895–1975)

63. Wash me throughly

Psalm 51: 2–3

David Halls
(b. 1963)

APPENDIX
(Other suitable easy anthems)

Abbreviations are used for the following, published or distributed by Oxford University Press:

Advent for Choirs	*AdfC*
Anthems for Choirs 1	*AfC 1*
Ash Wednesday to Easter for Choirs	*AWE*
Carols for Choirs	*CfC (1, 2 or 3)*
100 Carols for Choirs	*100 CfC*
The New Church Anthem Book	*NCAB*

Titles also available as separate leaflets are listed below as: *OUP*

TITLE	COMPOSER / ARRANGER	SOURCE
Advent		
Adam lay ybounden	Boris Ord	*CfC2*
Gabriel's message	arr. David Willcocks	*100 CfC*
Hail! Blessed Virgin Mary	arr. Charles Wood	*CfC2*
Lo, how a Rose e'er blooming	harm. M. Praetorius	*100 CfC*
On Jordan's bank	arr. Malcolm Archer	*AdfC*
Sleepers, wake!	Felix Mendelssohn	*AfC1*
This is the truth sent from above	arr. Vaughan Williams	*CfC2; 100 CfC*
Wachet auf	J. S. Bach	*AdfC*

Christmas and Epiphany
See *100 Carols for Choirs, Carols for Choirs* Volumes 1, 2, and 3, and the *Shorter New Oxford Book of Carols*

Lent and Passiontide		
A new commandment	Richard Shephard	*AWE*
Call to remembrance	Richard Farrant	*NCAB*
Comfort, O Lord, the soul of thy servant	William Crotch	*NCAB*
God so loved the world	John Goss	*NCAB*
God so loved the world	Bob Chilcott	*OUP*
Hide not thou thy face	Richard Farrant	*NCAB*

Palm Sunday		
The Feast of Palms	Alan Bullard	*AWE; OUP*

Easter		
He is risen	Percy Whitlock	*AWE*
Most glorious Lord of life	William H. Harris	*AWE*
Now the green blade riseth	arr. Simon Lindley	*AWE*
The day draws on with golden light	Edward Bairstow	*NCAB*
The strife is o'er	Henry G. Ley	*NCAB*

Ascension and Christ the King		
Above all praise and all majesty	Felix Mendelssohn	*NCAB*
Lord that descendedst, Holy Child	Eric Gritton	*AfC 1*

Pentecost

O Holy Spirit, Lord of grace	Christopher Tye	*NCAB*

Trinity

Hymn to the Trinity	Peter Ilich Tchaikovsky	*NCAB*

Saints Days

Give us the wings of faith	Ernest Bullock	*OUP*

Harvest

Look at the world	John Rutter	*OUP*
Praise, O praise	Martin How	*NCAB*

Funeral and Remembrance

God be in my head	Andrew Carter	*OUP*
God be in my head	John Rutter	*NCAB*
The souls of the righteous	Stanley Marchant	*NCAB*

Holy Communion

Ave verum corpus	William Byrd	*NCAB*
Ave verum corpus	Edward Elgar	*NCAB*

Annunciation and other Feasts of the BVM

Gabriel's message	arr. David Willcocks	*100 CfC*
Hail! Blessed Virgin Mary	arr. Charles Wood	*CfC2*

Baptism

Go forth into the world in peace	John Rutter	*OUP*

Wedding

The Lord bless you and keep you	John Rutter	*OUP*

General (including Thanksgiving/Praise)

A Clare Benediction	John Rutter	*OUP*
Almighty and everlasting God	Orlando Gibbons	*NCAB*
An Affirmation	Andrew Carter	*OUP*
Blest are the pure in heart	H. Walford Davies	*NCAB*
From the rising of the sun	F. A. Gore Ouseley	*AfC1*
Go before us, O Lord	Andrew Carter	*OUP*
Irish Blessing	Bob Chilcott	*OUP*
May the mystery of God enfold us	Andrew Carter	*OUP*
O gladsome light, O grace	Louis Bourgeois	*NCAB*
O praise the Lord	Adrian Batten	*OUP*
Praise to God in the Highest	S. S. Campbell	*OUP*
Psalm 150	John Harper	*OUP*
The Peace of God	David Willcocks	*OUP*

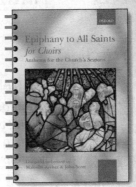
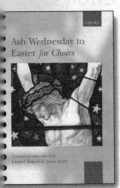

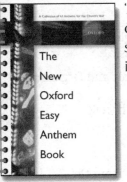